Learn Shapes With Buddy Bear

VOLUME 2

By Lavon I. Roberts

Learn Shapes With Buddy Bear
By Lavon I. Roberts

Meet **Buddy Bear!** He's going to teach you....

Buddy Bear wants to know...

What shape is this?

Circle

Buddy Bear wants to know...

What shape is this?

Square

Buddy Bear wants to know...

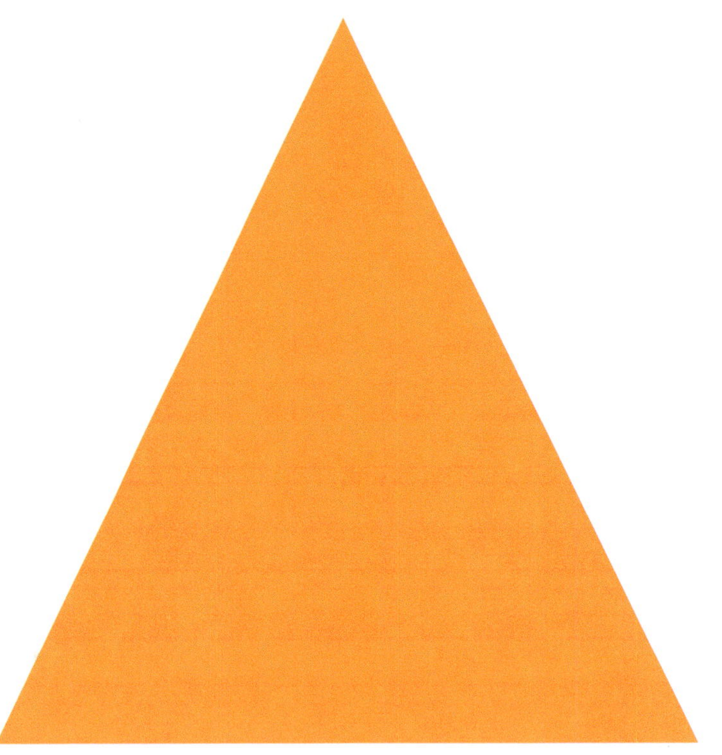

What shape is this?

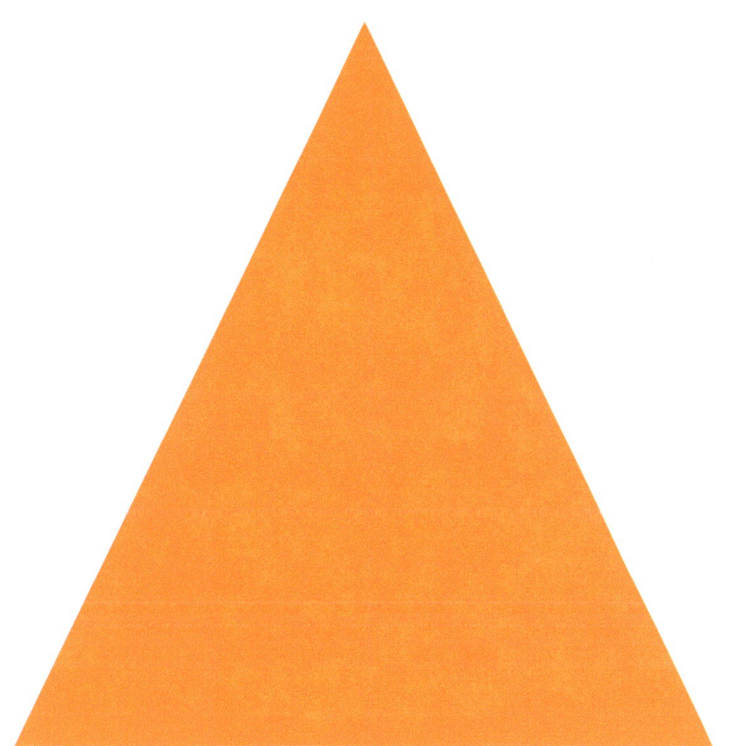

Triangle

Buddy Bear wants to know...

What shape is this?

Oval

Buddy Bear wants to know...

What shape is this?

Star

Buddy Bear wants to know...

What shape is this?

Rectangle

Buddy Bear wants to know... know...

What shape is this?

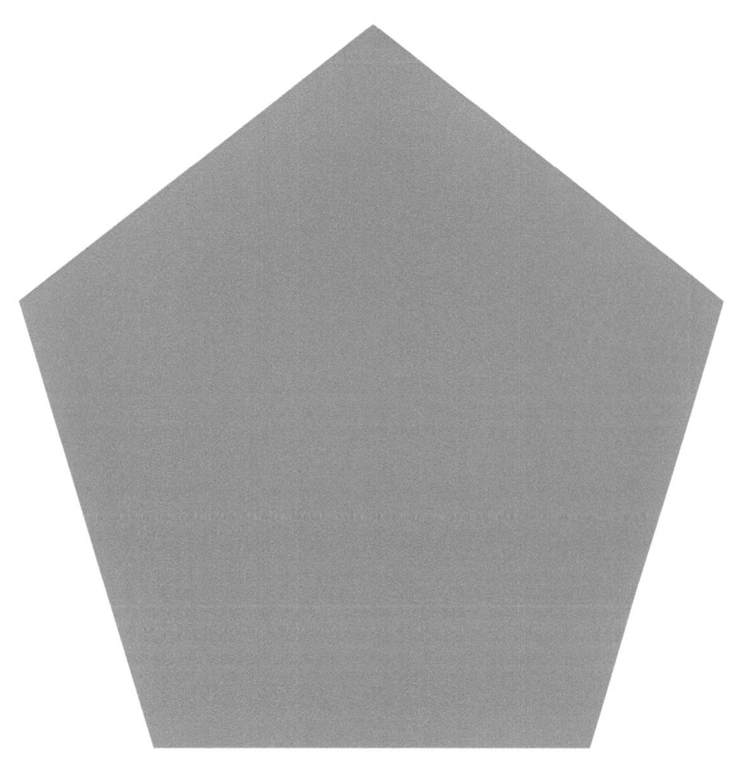

Pentagon

Buddy Bear wants to know...

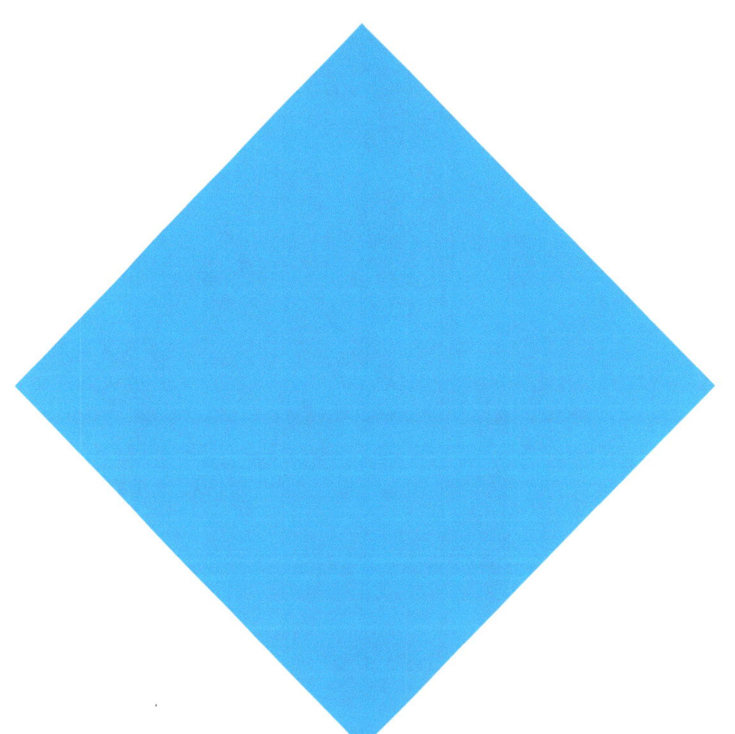

What shape is this?

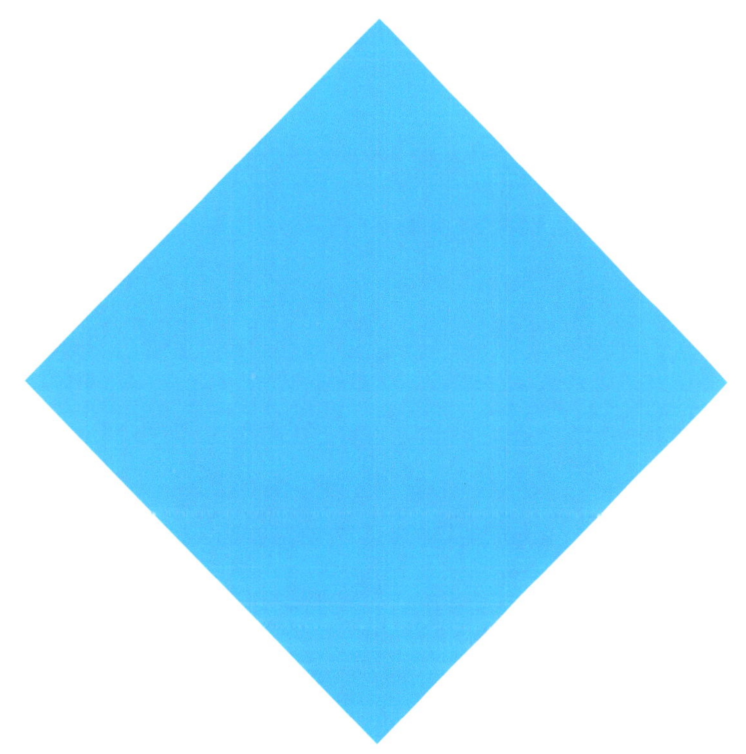

Diamond

Buddy Bear wants to know...

What shape is this?

Heart

Buddy Bear wants to know...

What shape is this?

# Cross

Buddy Bear wants to know...

What shape is this?

Hexagon

Buddy Bear wants to know...

What shape is this?

Parallelogram

Buddy Bear knows his Shapes!

Now, you do too!

More to come
From Buddy Bear
books....